MW01007969

Additional pr(

This debut volume places Danny Caine in the company of some of our best and most astute absurdist observers of 21st century popular culture: James Tate, Denise Duhamel, Mark Halliday and Nick Demske. When America goes on her book tour, Danny Caine must come along as translator.

—**George Bilgere,**
Author of *Blood Pages*

When was the last time you laughed and cried while reading poetry? Danny Caine's *Continental Breakfast* is a joyous all-you-can-eat buffet of suburban minivans, malls, bagels, Bud Lites, CompUSAs, Circuit Cities, Ford 150s, Applebee's, and Passover treats. Danny Caine is a voice so bold and hilarious you'll be telling all your all your friends (even the poetry-phobic ones): Buy this book. You won't regret it.

—**Kaitlyn Andrews-Rice,**
Editor-in-Chief of *Split Lip Magazine*

Danny Caine's *Continental Breakfast* portrays suburban life in the Midwest with humor, pathos, and tender care. You'll laugh, you'll cry, you'll raise your can of Bud Lite.

—**Megan Kaminski,**
Author of *Deep City*

LELE—

CONTINENTAL
BREAKFAST

Danny Caine

YOU ARE THE CERTIFIED BEST.
MAY EVERY EXIT HAVE
A WAFFLE HOUSE

Mason Jar Press | Baltimore, MD

Published and distributed by
Mason Jar Press
Baltimore, MD 21218

Printed by Spencer Printing in Honesdale, PA.

Learn more about Mason Jar Press at masonjarpress.xyz.

Index of poems, in order of appearance

Dedicated to Aunt Pat & Ms. Fitch

It would be difficult to overstate the men's enthusiasm for continental breakfast. To be clear, their zeal had little or nothing to do with this particular hotel's version of the standard spread. As petulant reviewers made very clear, the hotel's breakfast was not in any way exceptional or distinctive. It was a completely average continental breakfast, and this was why the men loved it.

—Chris Bachelder, The Throwback Special

I wouldn't live there if you paid me

—*Talking Heads, "The Big Country"*

Or something like that

—*Guided by Voices, "Echos Myron"*

CONTINENTAL
BREAKFAST

Where the streets have no name

JAYCIE

Darn girl the way you punch
those produce codes makes me want
to want to save myself for marriage.

Jaycie, check me out. Let me be
your bag boy, your paper plastic
knight. I wanna meet your mom,

I wanna see your old toy horses.
I'll show you my Eagle Scout badge
if you show me your Gold Award.

Whisper secret things to me, like
*have you considered accepting Jesus
Christ as your lord and savior?*

I'll make you latkes and teach you *all*
the Hanukkah blessings if you make me
a mix CD of your favorite Christian Rock

and call it *The GREATEST Love Songs Ever.*
After all, Jaycie, I'm vulnerable—I'm only
half, and we kind of do Christmas too.

Let's watch *Seventh Heaven* and eat
Baked Lays together under your
home ec blanket. Tell me

Danny Caine

I'm going to hell as you pull
my hand from the waistband
of your pajama pants.

#UPFORWHATEVER

Kyle, because we saw you
holding a bottle of Bud Lite we know
you're #UPFORWHATEVER happens—

why don't you go upstairs and see
how we SURPRISED YOU
with EMILY RATAJKOWSKI

wearing NOTHING BUT BUBBLES
in your MASTER SUITE.
What's that? You're worried

about what your wife will think?
Forget that shrill feminist! Look
on your desk—waiting for you

is a DOPE NEW STACK
of FRESH DIVORCE PAPERS.
All you have to do is sign on the line,

Kyle. Welcome to BUD LITE NATION
where MEN RUN FREE and your kids
have been shipped off to boarding school

FOR THE NEXT TEN YEARS
so they can't BUG their AWESOME
DAD at his NEW JOB with the FBI—

the FEMALE BODY INSPECTORS.
Kyle, don't even say it—*but I liked
my old job. I thought I was a pretty good*

second grade teacher. FUGGEDABOUTIT.
We sent LIAM NEESON to YOUR CLASSROOM
to tell the kiddos that Mr. Kyle was EXECUTED

by ISIS. He told them your LAST WORDS were
"DON'T FORGET YOUR SPELLING QUIZ
YOU LITTLE TURDS." Now you're FREE

to PLAY CALL OF DUTY ALL DAY. Thirsty?
We replaced your fridge with another fridge
SHAPED LIKE A BOTTLE OF BUD LITE

FILLED WITH BOTTLES OF BUD LITE!
Drank a bunch of Bud Lite? WE PUT
A URINAL IN EVERY ROOM.

No more sit-down pissing, yuppie boy.
Speaking of yuppie boy, look at those
PANSY TIGHT JEANS. Is there

even room for balls in there?
We replaced your ENTIRE WARDROBE
with BADASS BUD LITE GYM SHORTS.

We replaced your collection of family photos
with HI-DEFINITION PORTRAITS
of CONSTRUCTION EQUPIMENT.

You liked your little baby Honda? TOO BAD.
Say hello to your BUD LITE BLUE
HUMVEE. It's getting a fresh wax job

from a hottie named CANDY, who
also happens to be your PERSONAL
LIVE-IN BIKINI BACON CHEF.

Listen to you, Kyle. *It wasn't even my Bud Lite.*
My friend left it here. IT DOESN'T MATTER.
Holding ANY Bud Lite is a PASSPORT

to AWESOME. What do you mean,
please get out of my house? We'll leave
AS SOON AS YOU STOP CRYING,

GO TO THE FRIDGE, and
CRACK THE ICE-COLD BUD LIGHT
OF YOUR DESTINY.

DINNER AT APPLEBEE'S WITH EDWARD SAID

Don't give me that look, Edward. I know what
I want and I want an Oriental Chicken Salad.

I want to look around in chew-bliss and see Elvis,
a framed football jersey, and a goddamn trombone

all nailed to the fucking wall. I need flatscreens,
cocktails the color of highlighters, and to speak

the name of my desire without hearing you kvetch,
Edward. My grandmother made her grandmother's

fried chicken and my grandchildren will eat this
in these hightop swivel chairs. I'm trying to find a way

to think this doesn't suck and Edward, you're not helping.

BEN & JERRY'S FREE CONE DAY

Young lady I will indeed pay for my
Chunky Monkey. This is America—

there's no such thing as a free cone. Take
my money. I am paying you at a fair market

price for goods and services rendered because
that's how the whole system *works*. No

it's *not* a tip. Don't even get me started on tipping.
You give me stuff, I give you money. I sure as hell

didn't earn my family's first college degree by way
of gratis desserts. No I will not step aside, and do not

sir me. I don't care if there's a line. I'll be happy to leave
after you do your job as a cashier, as a *citizen*, and get paid

by me. The America my dad stormed Normandy for
is built on hard work, not handouts. You know what?

Fine. Keep your Chunky Monkey. Go to hell Ben,
and you too Jerry. Take your commie cone day

to Cuba or China or Brooklyn or something,
just get it out of my country.

THE BEST LITTLE PASTA
PLACE IN FLORENCE

is at the corner of won't say and not telling
because if I did you'd just call in to the Rick
Steves Show, and he'd put it in his little book
and then all the doddering American aunts
and uncles would dodder to this perfect restaurant
by the goddamn busload and when I figure out how
to get back to Italy I won't be the only one
in my Best Little Pasta Place in Florence
speaking English.
                          And I mean that "my."
This place belongs to just me and these *locals*
with local cigarettes and local tans and local
quirky Italian hospitality! If I can have just this,
I'll behave myself otherwise. I'll be a good little tourist,
using my fold-out map and my closed-toed feet
to keep to the pre-approved route:
Ufizzi—Duomo—Academia—Ponte Vecchio
in sensible breathable pants because the internet
says Italian men don't wear shorts.
                          My pants swish
Eddie Bauerly as I walk towards you know where, and
I can already taste the peppery and succulent ▮▮▮▮▮,
feel the ice cold ▮▮▮▮ ▮▮▮▮ sliding down my throat.
All this plus complimentary ▮▮▮▮ for a mere €▮▮!
I walk faster and turn the corner from Via ▮▮▮▮ onto

Via ███████ and I see it, a barely marked doorway right
past the spraypainted scrawl that says, "Yankee go home."

IN THE BATHROOM OF THE
RENAISSANCE DOWNTOWN

*"Access to the hotel is policed by a series of signs
that constantly remind you that if you look a little
funny—a little down on your luck, say, or a little
ragged around the edges—then this isn't the place
for you."*

—Juliana Spahr, Well Then There Now

Hey fuck you automatic faucet—
no matter what your shitty laser
eye thinks, I am a person
covered in a body with hands

covered in putrid soap that
another shitty laser eye ejaculated
onto them and here *you* are ignoring
me while somehow making me feel

unclean. On, you sullen stainless robot.
I don't want the guy with the mouthwash
and mints to see me thrashing soapy hands
below your unblinking eye. Whose idea

was it to put lasers on faucets, anyway?
Is it another way to rid the Renaissance

of riffraff? It's like you know I'm more
Fairfield Inn than Ritz, that I'd rather

whoosh through a laser door
(and *those* lasers always see me)
than have one opened for me
by a dude in a silly hat. What about

the people who have to pee but are
more Super 8 than Fairfield? More crashing
on their brother's couch than Super 8?
People who open their own doors?

People who never go through doors at all?
Do your North Carolina cousins demand
birth certificates before turning on?
My friend is convinced you all ignore him

because his palms are dark. Fuck you
and fuck this place and fuck the politics
of pissing downtown, where bathrooms
are reserved for *paying customers* or

people who can get over feeling like
a third grader long enough to ask
for the keys please at the desk. How
many doors, how many times

did I have to prove my jeans
were nice enough before I could be
permitted entry to this marbled
echo vault where all I can see

is myself
in a spotless wall-sized mirror
while you refuse to see me
or my silent soapy prayer?

FOUR FRIARS, EACH ALIKE IN DIGNITY, IN FAIR WASHINGTON DC

I get rush tickets for a performance
of *Romeo and Juliet* and I'm killing
time before the show just sitting
in the back row looking at the set—
a kind of CONTEMPORARY
abandoned banquet hall with stacks
of those gold chairs from every
semi-classy wedding reception.
All of a sudden, in walks one
two three four *friars*, actual friars
in white robes and beads and sandals
and everything. I didn't know they
still made friars. But it makes sense—
I bet friars love *Romeo and Juliet*
the way Wookiees love *Star Wars*.
The house is still mostly empty,
basically just me staring
at a row of buzzed heads rising from
white hooded shoulders in a theater
shoved into a row of gentrified
garbage restaurants, fusion places
with singular noun names, 15 dollar
tableside guacamole service, industrial
salvage shit all over neon uplit cinderblock
and leatherbound menus you can't even

read because those damn filament bulbs
don't actually do anything. Outside
orange VALET cones blocking
every spot in front of one of those
DIGNIFIED Starbucks you see
in buildings with tall windows and
banners declaring THIS IS THE
PLACE FOR DISTINGUISHED
URBAN LIVING AVAILABLE
NOW WITH UNITS STARTING
at a number that takes me 10 years
to even think about let alone earn.
In other words no place for a goddamn
friar—sorry for my language, gentlemen.
Just ignore me. I hope the guy they got
to play your man tonight is good.
I hope you wince in delighted horror
as act four treads into unfriarlike
moral territory. Then, stand and clap
till your hands hurt and slowly walk
back into that unholy night.

THE IDEAL BUDWEISER CUSTOMER
WATCHES A BUDWEISER COMMERCIAL

Oh shit I love "Landslide."
I was going to get up to piss but then
I heard me some Fleetwood Mac.
Hey that's a pretty farm, too. Farms are dope.
Wait, oh goddamn, it's a *baby horse*
lying in some *fucking* sawdust.

That baby horse is so cute I can't even
handle it right now. I am *literally*
unsure how to proceed. And now the horse
is being fed from a *bottle*? The hell am I supposed to do
with that? Dammit now the horse and the dude
are playing and stuff. Fuck me if I don't love
a playful goddamn horse.
Look! A Budweiser truck. Budweiser!

I should like this brand on Facebook.
I should follow this brand on Twitter.
I really should make an effort to engage
with this brand on social media.

Wait, that's a *horse* trailer. And our dude
is shaking hands with the driver? Is he—

DUDE YOU CAN'T SELL THAT FUCKING HORSE!

YOU'RE GOING TO MISS HIM SO MUCH!
He's your FROLICKING BUDDY!

What the HELL, bro?
Bum me out.

Uh-oh: CLYDESDALE PARADE! In a CITY!

And there's our guy! And could that possibly be—

aww MAN the horse didn't see our dude
because he's wearing blinders.

This commercial makes me want to die.

BUT WAIT.
YOU PUT THAT FORD F150 KING RANCH
BACK IN PARK THIS INSTANT

BECAUSE HERE COMES YOUR HORSE
in SLOW MO HD GALLOPING
DOWN the FUCKING STREET

because he *remembered* you.

Somebody get me a Budweiser.

IF THE CAVS WIN THE NBA TITLE

The potholes will fill themselves. Clam chowder,
cheesecake, pizza, and hot dogs will all be served
Cleveland style, everywhere. Johnny Manziel
will drink nothing but orange juice and do nothing
but practice and whittle wooden toy trains
for Make-A-Wish kids. Weekends we'll watch Tina Fey say
LIVE FROM CLEVELAND, IT'S SATURDAY NIGHT.
The Indians will replace Chief Wahoo with
a rainbow. The steel plants will roar back to life
to fill the demand for Lebron James statues.
Graduation rates at Cleveland City Schools will climb
to 105%. After the police sponsored whoopie-cushion-
for-handgun exchange program drops the homicide
rate to almost nothing, all the cop cars will be painted
pink and emblazoned with BLACK LIVES MATTER
or THIS IS WHAT A FEMINIST LOOKS LIKE.
On Halloween people will hand out full-time jobs
instead of candy. Tower City will get an Ikea and
the casino will become another art museum.
Obama will open his presidential library here
and then coach the Browns to the Super Bowl.
Paris will rename itself "New Cleveland." Idealistic
southern kids will run away from home hitchhiking
with a sign that says "Cleveland or bust." The city
will shine and the buildings will sing and the sun
will never set. It'll only snow on Christmas.

If the Cavs win the finals, Cleveland
will be 72, sunny, unrecognizable.

CHRISSY, JOHN, KANYE, AND KIM GO TO WAFFLE HOUSE

"Nobody bothered them. They ate, they had fun. They danced a little. We have a jukebox in here."

—Carolyn Washington, manager of some Waffle House in Phoenix

Nobody bothered them. They ate, they had fun.
Someone commented on how clean the bathrooms were.
They danced a little. Every Waffle House has a Jukebox.
Kanye wouldn't look at Kim. John and Chrissy held hands.

John checked if the bathrooms locked from inside.
Kim said, "isn't there a Pavement album called Smothered
    Covered something?"
Kanye said, "are you speaking English?" John and Chrissy
    had disappeared.
Kim said, "oh Kanye you're so cute when you're hangry."

Kim ordered hashbrowns smothered, covered, and capped.
Chrissy sat down, wiped her lips, and ordered a Diet Coke.
Kim said, "Chrissy isn't Kanye cute when he's hangry?"
Kanye sank into a thousand-waffle stare.

Chrissy nodded and downed her Diet Coke in a few gulps.
Kanye treaded water in his thousand-waffle stare—

He wondered what would happen if he abandoned all of them.
They looked like people in a bad movie about ordinary people.

When the waffles arrived, Kanye pooled the syrup and ate
 with abandon.
Against John's cheek Chrissy whispered, "every house
 should be a Waffle House."
John and Chrissy danced to their song ("Ordinary People").
Nobody bothered them. They ate. They had fun.

ENGLISH 102 IN BIG 12 COUNTRY

In a town like this the games
screen in the movie theater: I watch
a 20-foot tall version of the already tall
shooting guard from my 12:00 class
sink a three. Cheer, spill popcorn, forget
that he has not turned in his second essay.

He's projected to go first round
in this year's NBA draft, meaning
he's staring down $2,288,200 and I'm
asking him to care about a literacy narrative.
Just how far is the essay from his mind
with this conference game slipping
away, 2:20 left and no fouls to give?

He probably won't show up tomorrow.
His classmates and his teacher and most
of the citizens of his time-being town
watch as our Legendary Head Coach smacks
his ass. We read lips: WHAT THE FUCK
WAS THAT. He fouls out. They lose.
The theater empties quietly. We can hear

the traffic lights change. Townies curse
his name under breath. My wife asks
if I'm okay while I try to not to be

the distant sports fan spouse.
At least when Lebron James makes me
a bad husband, I don't have to
teach him thesis statements.

BONO RINGS MY DOORBELL

All is quiet.

"I know you're in there," Bono says. "I saw the blinds move.
Just open the door and let me give you our new record

for free." "Go away," I say. "I can't," he says. "Why not," I say.
He says, "I still haven't found what I'm looking for—

what I'm looking for is getting this record to as many
people as possible." He rings the doorbell again.

"Danny there's no use hiding," he says. "I will follow
you until you take it," he says. "I will follow."

I say, "How the fuck do you know my name?" He says,
"I move in mysterious ways." I say, "that's not funny."

He says, "in the name of love open the door."
I say, "not funny either." He tries the knob.

I jam a chair against the door. He tries
the knob again, harder. I call the cops.

I tell the dispatcher what's going on. She says,
"the album is actually pretty good." I text Kara

and tell her I'm safe, I'll be in touch soon. I grab
my favorite box of 45s and crawl out the window

into the backyard and run. It's a beautiful day
and I want to run. I want to hide. I want to tear down

the walls that hold me inside. And when I go there,
I'll go there without you and without your stupid record,

Bono, to a place where the streets do have fucking names.

CONTINENTAL BREAKFAST

All the waffles in Texas
are shaped like Texas. All
the waffles in Ohio
are shaped like waffles.

At your basic Towne Place Suites
expect egg patties with fake
yellow yolks. Spring Hill Suites
go for "scrambled" "eggs"—

nothing a Tabasco bath
can't fix. In the Colorado Springs
Hampton Inn parking lot
my boy scout troop looked up,

third floor window: a volleyball team
showing us their cotton underwear.
They closed the curtains, laughing.
I missed it, was looking somewhere

else. Never get in line for waffles
behind a family with more than
two children. A Residence Inn
will rotate two hot dishes:

turkey sausage patties, biscuits,
or this pretty good homefries stuff
with peppers and onions. In the
Pasadena La Quinta I accidentally

kissed Tina after a power hour
with Mike's Hard Limeade 40s
because neither of us liked
beer yet. In the morning

she cried by the juice machine.
The key to those little milks is really
squeezing hard before you push up.
At the Best Western in Nashville

breakfast is in the bar—my brother
loved this as much as he loved watching
last night's sad Stetson strumming
a Telecaster for tips in the same room.

At the Garden City AmericInn I
spent most of Christmas night watching
Chip and Joanna as Applebee's
lights bled through the blackouts.

How many yogurts can you fit
in your purse, and how far down
I-70 before they turn? At the Super 8
in Clearfield, Kara told me to look

at the parking lot billboard rabbits
but I just kept watching the *Too Cute*
marathon. Later that year we got married
in a Hyatt. For rest stop or for offramp,

in hunger and in saran-wrapped
red delicious apples and bananas
if I'm lucky. Toast the English muffin,
put the sausage and egg patty in it,

then put the whole thing in a napkin
in your pocket. I may not know
much but I know it's five hours
to Terre Haute and they've got

a pretty good Fazoli's. I may not know much
but I did stay at a Holiday Inn Express last night.

Where the streets do have fucking names

INTERSECTION OF COTTESMORE
AND TALLYHO

God said name the streets after English foxhunting shit and let every family have 3/4 acres and a narrow woods in the backyard, and it was night and it was morning: the first day. And God said let the parents watch HGTV to learn words like open concept subway tile backsplash kitchen island two car attached garage, and it was night and it was morning, the second day. And God said let the parents build big houses with open concept subway tile backsplash kitchen island two car attached garage children, and it was night and it was morning the third day. God said let a highway connect this town with the next town with the next town with the city to the north so the town's fathers may have easy commutes; let every offramp have an Applebee's and let every Applebee's have a parking lot and let every Applebee's parking lot have a Bob Evans too, and it was night and it was morning: the fourth day. And God said let the corporation that makes airplane bags of peanuts level a dairy farm to build a factory; let the factory pay property taxes to fund the schools; let the schools earn Super Excellent Plus on every year's state report card; let every senior take 5 AP classes, and it was night and it was morning: the fifth day. And God said let the children hate it here, and it was night and it was morning the sixth day. And God said let the children *totally can't wait to get out of here*; let the children graduate college and move to the cities their parents fled to come here; let the parents move further south after their foxhunty property values go down; in every generation let this cycle repeat; let not the mansions crumble, let not the children stay away, if only on the holidays.

SONG OF MY SUBURB

Pour one out for Blockbuster.
Pour one out for Borders.
Pour one out for the old
Giant Eagle where we'd linger
under parking lot LEDs after
Applebee's half price apps.
Pour one out for our Applebee's.
Pour one out for Circuit City
that turned into Best Thrift
that turned into an empty
Circuit City-shaped building.
Pour one out for Dana's old
driveway where I kissed her
across the armrests in her
mom's minivan and she
laughed at me. Pour one
out for all the abandoned
minivans somewhere in
minivan heaven or where-
ever they go after the kids
go to college. Pour one out
for the empty CVS that
used to be a full CVS that
used to be another cornfield

next to another cornfield
where I once got a kiss
and a fairly serious rash.
Do it. Invert your Code
Red Mountain Dew. Pour
out your blue Powerade.
Pour out your stripmall heart
onto this asphalt, onto the spaces
way out by the sidewalks that
never fill except when buried
under mountains of brown snow.

I LOVE YOU DETROIT

for Dan Gilbert

I love you Detroit
People Mover because you don't give
a fuck you just give rides

to people like me, bloated
with Saganaki, dragging on escalators
through casino clatter to find

a monorail of all things waiting
to go on a three mile clockwise loop
of the theaters and parking garages

and a parking garage that was once
a theater. Halfway through the Renaissance
Center clears its throat and asks me:

When did people begin imagining
automated trains or international airports,
or automated trains inside international airports

or a train that goes nowhere and costs
$4 per rider mile in a city choking
on its own bones?

Ride, the Ren Cen tells me. Ride
and I glide through her shadow thinking
something in Detroit must keep moving.

LEFT ON FALCON, RIGHT ON GRISSOM

Invisible flight suit walk to my rental
Mustang: Bruce Springsteen is already
cued up and I've set the interior
ambient lighting to red (this car is so
manly you can make its inside bleed
with the push of a button). Watch me
roar a muscle car in a driveway outside
a shitty Airbnb. Watch me turn left
on Falcon and right on Grissom
and right onto the Causeway
in the morning mist punctured
by weird plants and frogsound
inaudible over the Boss. This dusty
beach road leads to skeleton frames
of burned out Saturn Vs. Watch my
speed or don't. Watch the horizon
for the VAB, the shuttle, the goddamn
rockets, man. The Eagle has landed.

Yesterday I walked down the street
to get shrimp and sangria.
Nobody told me nobody walks
in Florida but it was close enough
that walking was easier than two lefts.
From a hotel portico two whitebeards
in bermudas shouted at me and I got

all tense. Fight or flight. This was
Florida, after all. They yelled again.
No, no guns tucked into waistbands.
They were saying *rocket*. They hoisted
their Coronas, extended fingers
to the horizon, to the column
of smoke reaching to the sky.

THE NEW AMERICAN DREAM

The Borders is closed.
the Borders are all closed.
The walls still stand but
the Borders are no longer
open. The old Borders
is wearing a Halloween
Store costume, with vinyl
"Spirit Halloween" banners
over labelscar and awnings
frayed and waving like
a mummy costume's arms.
They're called Ghostboxes,
these walls that used
to signify Borders and
Circuit Cities and CompUSAs
all across these United States.
The American dream:
buy a ghost in a box
in a Ghostbox anywhere
walls but not Borders rise
from parking lot shining
seas. Step here to see
something scary.

NOT A POEM ABOUT A PARKING GARAGE

I drove to Detroit to see
a friend and write a poem
about a parking garage
that was once a theater

and its Cadillac corridors
under arching proscenium,
but then I drove past
its entrance signs—

NO TRESSPASSING,
PRIVATE PROPERTY,
and an angry, hand-scrawled
DO NOT WALK IN

directed to people like me,
iPhone camera in hand
to catalogue fallen splendor
and all that but the garage

covered its private parts.
It did not cower. It said yes
I was a theater, and now I am
a parking garage. It's none

of your business. No I did not
go in. What would I have said
anyway? Detroit is bankrupt and
this parking garage is Coleman Young?

A man sat down across from me
on the People Mover and shook
my hand. I asked him what was new
in Detroit. He said everything.

GUN MATH

add brother add brother add house
subtract mother years ago add father
still at work add his gun add accident

add announcement during homeroom
add hole in the seating chart add
counselor in the lunchroom add
counselor in the teacher lunchroom
add suits add car flags add handshake line
add year off for the brother who remains

add questions: what do I say
to the father over our first handshake—
that I just started teaching so my only
significant memory is busting him
for plagiarism before he became
a hole in my seating chart, a hole
in his family? What do I say
to the people who want me to change
the seating chart? The people who don't?

I was a teacher—I was supposed
to have the answers. I taught English,
not math, but I'll give this a shot—
do not subtract father, do not subtract
even more sons, do not subtract house,
I guess that leaves a gun.

ONE-STAR TRIPADVISOR REVIEWS
OF THE MEMPHIS BASS PRO

This should be my kind of paradise but it's not. Amazing building, but after walking several blocks along Front Street we never did find the key to the entrance. I am not a hunter, a fisherman or an outdoorsman so I don't know what I was thinking. If you're an actual Bass Pro shopper, don't go to this store. For a real "Bass Pro Experience" go to Springfield! I love guns. I was only there to buy one box of ammo. I LOVE Bass Pro Shops, when driving across the country there was no way I could pass this one up. I could use another holster. We could have just gone to see Santa in Hot Springs near where we live but my five-year-old thinks that the real Santa lives here at Bass Pro. I was answered with a shrug of the shoulders by a very uninterested hostess. The people you choose to employ will be your demise, leaving yet another building to close. I had a few items to purchase, which I thought about putting back after the bad experience, but I really liked the items. Shame on you, Bass Pro. Thankfully my husband shared one of his 3 pimento cheeseburgers.

LOCKDOWN

Blake got shifty during lockdown drills.
Not the imagined gunman, the real
drug dogs snarling the halls. With
the right class, one that can get through
a lockdown without fucking off, you could
hear the sniffs. Once, a bark. Lights off,
curtains closed. The doors only locked
from the outside. One year we had to open
the door, hand out with a key, and twist.
Blake often disappeared for a few days
after lockdowns. The next year we forgot
the doors and worried about ringtones.
Kids disappeared a lot. The principal
had a different strategy every year. Throw
a desk through the windows and run.
The principal never told us why the kids
disappeared. Cover the slit window
in the door with construction paper.
First Taylor and Third Taylor both
disappeared. A runner came to fetch
Michael for the office. Michael wouldn't
get up. The runner shrugged and left.
One year, a set of code names to recite
over the PA. *Unless the message comes
from Wildcat, ignore it. Do not tell this
to the students.* The principal came to

the door—*Michael, it's time to come to
my office.* Michael's eyes iced. Principal:
*Danny, take your class for a walk. If you
see Coach Murphy, send him down here.*
Tori disappeared twice, before and after
the essay she said was fiction about her dad
throwing her down the stairs. I wondered
about every window. I wondered about
every sweatshirt. Guns, sure, but also
scratches. Bruises. Bellies. Sometimes I
looked in the window and saw threats.
Sometimes, in the winter, when 6:30
looked like ink, I looked in the windows
and saw only myself in an empty classroom.

CHURCHES REPLACING STORES AT EUCLID SQUARE MALL (WITH SLIDESHOW)

Diamond Company:
A church. Bank One:
A church. Foot Locker

A church. Foot Locker
now folding chair rows—
Father, Son, Holy Ghost.

Father, Son, and Holy
Ghostbox: What do you
want, flying buttresses?

No flying buttresses here,
just frayed sunfade banners.
Nutcracker. Dry fountain.

Dry fountain. Nutcracker.
I could get ruin porny—
18 creepiest photos,

25 spookiest pics of
the abandoned empty
Euclid Square Mall.

But Euclid Square Mall
is already documented—
decrepit, dead, dying.

Dead, dying, decrepit
on the internet; on
Sundays it's resurrected.

Sundays it's resurrected—
At least I assume so.
It wasn't when I went.

When I went it was
Empty and echoing,
the locks drilled out.

The locks drilled out
under signs warning
Unaccompanied teens

that unaccompanied teens
aren't allowed. Nothing
about unaccompanied poets

or unaccompanied poets
turning their notebooks
into internet slideshows.

Internet slideshow poems
of creepy images to eat.
I've learned, eating a ghost.

I've learned eating a ghost
isn't filling, so I try to see
that people go to church.

That people go to church
here, that they can forget
that this space isn't,

that this space wasn't
sacred, that someone
in theory can look and see

in theory can look and see
not old stores, not death. Not
Diamond Company. Church.

INTERSTATE LOVE SONG

for Kara

When we get to Cracker Barrel
    stiff and cold
you can have the seat closest
    to the fire
and first crack at the peg game.
    You can even
have the third biscuit.
    At hour 13
I'll do anything to keep you
    awake and
laughing and pointed west.
    I don't need
anything from you except
    your body
in the seat next to mine
    going 75.
I don't need anything
    from you
except the promise
    you'll go
somewhere else with me
    whenever
we feel like it. Let's play
    the license plate

game. Let's play the alphabet
    game until
we get stuck on J. Let's play
    the game
where America is the board,
    the mile markers
are tokens, the God billboards
    are bonuses,
the rollergrill hotdogs are penalties,
    and we're on
the same team beating everyone.
    Tomorrow
let's take hotel coffee to go
    and shiver
our way through Dinosaur World.
    Fuck flowers,
I'll buy you a purple triceratops.
    Anyone can
fall in love in Paris.

THE MIDDLE WEST

In our story we're as connected as the Pizza Hut and Arby's parking lots. In our story we're as connected as Burbank Road and Burbank Road's Frontage Road. In our story we're as connected as $2 Margarita night and the Mexican place between Goodwill and the nicer Wal-Mart.

Our story from speakers that look like rocks. Our story scooped into fake velvet bags of souvenir gems. Our story in food poisoning from Sbarro's Pizza. Our story at Giant Eagle past midnight because it's the only place still open.

Our story landlocked our story landlines' curly cords in grandma's house, 1976 Christmas Run Drive. Our story not in brownstones or bodegas or beaches or commuter trains. In our story Subways sell sandwiches and the Skyline is chili.

Our story at an Irish Pub in Scranton where the bartender loses our tab so we get eight beers and a souvenir glass for six bucks. In our story we go under a barricade and climb wood stairs to the roof as a 90s cover band hacks through "Say It Ain't So." Through fogs of our breath we tell our story to each other.

Index of buildings, in order of appearance

JAYCIE

Heinen's Fine Foods, 10049 Darrow Rd, Twinsburg, OH 44087

DINNER AT APPLEBEE'S WITH EDWARD SAID

Applebee's, 6140 Som Center Rd, Solon, OH 44139 (permanently closed)

BEN & JERRY'S FREE CONE DAY

Ben & Jerry's, 20650 N Park Blvd, University Heights, OH 44118

THE BEST LITTLE PASTA PLACE IN FLORENCE

Osteria ███████, Piazza ████████, ███, ███ Florence, Italy

IN THE BATHROOM OF THE RENAISSANCE DOWNTOWN

Renaissance, 225 3rd Ave S, Minneapolis, MN 55401

**FOUR FRIARS, EACH ALIKE IN DIGNITY, IN FAIR
WASHINGTON, DC**

Shakespeare Theater Company, 450 7th St NW, Washington, DC 20004

IF THE CAVS WIN THE NBA TITLE

JACK Casino, Tower City Center, 100 Public Square, Cleveland, OH 44113

CHRISSY, JOHN, KANYE, AND KIM GO TO WAFFLE HOUSE

Waffle House, 1237 N 59th Ave, Phoenix, AZ 85043 (permanently closed)

ENGLISH 102 IN BIG 12 COUNTRY

Liberty Hall, 644 Massachusetts St, Lawrence, KS 66044

CONTINENTAL BREAKFAST

TownePlace Suites, 525 N 2nd St, Minneapolis, MN 55401

SpringHill Suites, 1421 Olentangy River Rd, Columbus, OH 43212

Hampton Inn, 7245 Commerce Center Dr., Colorado Springs, CO 80919

Residence Inn, 1620 SW Westport Dr, Topeka, KS 66604

La Quinta, 3490 East Sam Houston Pkwy S, Pasadena, TX 77505

Best Western Plus, 1407 Division St, Nashville, TN 37203

AmericInn, 3020 E Kansas Ave, Garden City, KS 67846

Super 8, 14597 Clearfield Shawville Hwy, Clearfield, PA 16830

Hyatt, 420 Superior Avenue East, Cleveland, OH, USA, 44114

Fazoli's, 2940 S 3rd St, Terre Haute, IN 47802

AT THE INTERSECTION OF COTTESMORE AND TALLYHO, SOLON, OHIO

House, █████ Cottesmore Ln, Solon, OH 44139 (permanently closed)

SONG OF MY SUBURB

Blockbuster, 34362 Aurora Rd, Solon, OH 44139 (permanently closed)

Borders, 6025 Kruse Dr, Solon, OH 44139 (permanently closed)

Giant Eagle, 34310 Aurora Rd, Solon, OH 44139 (permanently closed)

Applebee's, 6140 Som Center Rd, Solon, OH 44139 (permanently closed)

Circuit City, 21639 Miles Rd, North Randall, OH 44128 (permanently closed)

CVS, 10085 Darrow Rd, Twinsburg, OH 44087

I LOVE YOU DETROIT

Greektown Casino, 555 E Lafayette St, Detroit, MI 48226

Renaissance Center, 400 Renaissance Center, Detroit, MI 48243

LEFT ON FALCON, RIGHT ON GRISSOM

John F. Kennedy Space Center, Florida, 32899

Breakwater Hotel at the Beach, 2707 Sadler Rd, Fernandina Beach, FL 32034

THE NEW AMERICAN DREAM

Borders/Spirit Halloween, 700 New Hampshire St, Lawrence, KS 66044 (permanently closed)

NOT A POEM ABOUT A PARKING GARAGE

The Michigan Theater, 220 Bagley Ave, Detroit, MI 48226 (permanently closed)

GUN MATH

 High School, ▆▆▆▆▆▆▆▆ ▆▆▆▆▆, OH ▆▆▆▆ (Permanently Closed)

ONE-STAR MEMPHIS TRIPADVISOR REVIEWS

Bass Pro Shops at the Pyramid, 1 Bass Pro Dr, Memphis, TN 38105

CHURCHES REPLACING STORES AT EUCLID SQUARE MALL (WITH SLIDESHOW)

Euclid Square Mall, 100 Euclid Square Mall, Euclid, OH 44132 (permanently closed).

Note: in 2017, Euclid Square Mall was leveled to make space for an Amazon fulfillment warehouse.

LOCKDOWN

See entry for "Gun Math."

INTERSTATE LOVE SONG

Cracker Barrel, 800 Happy Valley St, Cave City, KY 42127

Dinosaur World, 711 Mammoth Cave Rd, Cave City, KY 42127

THE MIDDLE WEST

El Campesino, 177 W Milltown Rd # C, Wooster, OH 44691

Walmart Supercenter, 3883 Burbank Rd, Wooster, OH 44691

Kildaire's Irish Pub, 119 Jefferson Ave, Scranton, PA 18503

UNCLE HAROLD'S
MAXWELL HOUSE HAGGADAH

KADESH

[We say the Kiddush]
[First glass of wine]

WE RAISE THE FIRST GLASS AND SAY

Let all who are hungry come and eat. Let all who are in need come and celebrate Passover. This year we are here, next year in Jerusalem and *this year* Maxwell House hired an ad agency to convince a rabbi to declare coffee Kosher For Passover and *this year* Maxwell House started giving away Haggadahs with cans of coffee and *this year* I actually tried to keep Kosher and ate Matzoh Pizza with pepperoni every night.

This year Aunt Lisa bought the Rite Lite® Ten Plagues Toy Kit and *this year* Uncle Harold downloaded the Passover PowerPoint and *this year* Uncle Harold and Aunt Lisa screamed at each other in the living room and *this year* Grandma gave everyone only two ice cubes and *this year* we never forget: only two ice cubes.

This year Grandpa married the much-younger shiksa and *this year* Grandpa didn't show up and *this year* Uncle Harold became Sedermeister and *this year* Grandpa had a fall and some heart stuff and so began his apology tour and so began his return.

This year we got new Haggadahs and *this year* we tread lightly in the house because Aunt Lisa died there and *this* year we did the toy plagues anyway and *this year* Uncle Harold introduced us to his new girlfriend and *this year* Uncle Harold sold his house.

This year I started writing poems about us and *this year* we took away Grandma's car and *this year* grandma died and *this year* one of the grandchildren had children and *this year* Uncle Harold became Grandfather Harold and *this year* I moved to Kansas and *this year* I didn't go to the Seder and *this year we are here, next year in Jerusalem,* or at least Cleveland, at least Uncle Harold's folding chairs.

THE INFLATABLE MATZOH
BALL OF AFFLICTION

*Wherefore is this night distinguished from all
other nights? Any other night we may eat
either leavened or unleavened bread, but on this night only*
Wavy Lay's Kosher for Passover.

and our children and our children's children
will have Bissli Pizza Flavor Party Snack
and Manischevitz Fruity Magic Loops Cereal.

because it is written:
in the Maxwell House Haggadah—

This is the bread of affliction
and the Passover Coke of affliction,
and the Rite Lite Inflatable Matzoh Ball of affliction,
and the Manischevitz Milk Chocolate Lollycones of
affliction.

*Baruch Atah Adonai, Eloheinu Melech haolam,
Borei p'ri Manischevitz*

Blessed art thou, O Lord, our God, who createst
Manischevitz American Concord Grape
Specially Sweetened
Containing Not Less than 51% Concord Wine—
and Kedem Grape Juice for the shiksa girlfriend.

MITZVAH ALEINU L'SAPER
BIYTZIYAT MITZRAYIM.
[It is a commandment upon us to tell
of the exodus from Egypt]

Mitzvah aleinu not l'saper Biytziyat Grandpa
[We do not tell of Grandpa's exodus]
[Uncle Harold is Sedermeister now]
[the divorce already gave Grandma one stroke]

Mitzvah
[barks at something in the backyard]

Uncle Harold
[yells at Mitzvah]
[rises to wash his hands]

Ur'Chatz
[we are supposed to wash our hands too]
[only Uncle Harold does]

L'Hadlik ner Shel Yom Tov
[the candles are lit]
[did I miss the blessing?]
[do we even do that one?]

Aleinu to recline in our chairs
    [only Uncle Harold does]
    [the wicked son does too]
    [his is a slouching adolescence]

Aleinu
    [to spill the manischevitz on the white lace]

Mitzvah Aleinu L'saper
    [the Seder must run 30 minutes]
    [no more, no less]
    [even Grandpa knew this]
    [in Uncle Harold's Maxwell House Haggadah]
    [you can still see the highlights]

Mitzvah Aleinu L'saper
    [we take turns reading]
    [visitors too]
    [even the girlfriend]
    [she can read the parts with the Hebrew names]
    [listen to her trip over *Gamliel, Eliazar, Yocheved*]

MAGGID

[we tell the story of Passover]
[we tell the story of Exodus]
[second glass of wine]

WE RAISE THE SECOND GLASS AND SAY

We praise you, Adonai our God, Ruler of the Universe,
Who has freed us and our ancestors from Egypt
and brought us to Cleveland

this night to eat matzoh and maror. Adonai,
our God and God of our ancestors, help us
celebrate future holidays
in Cleveland and Cleveland alone
or Jerusalem, I guess
but not New York
or Kansas
or Columbus
or Las Vegas.

Adonai our God Help us celebrate future holidays
and festivals in peace and in joy
and not in diminishing numbers—

Then we will thank you with a new song,
l'chayim.

THE SEVEN PLAGUES I COULD FIND

When we recall these plagues, we remove a toy, each a symbol of joy, from our Rite Lite Ten Plagues Kit®, because the deliverance of our people from the hands of the Egyptians was 25% off last year. Together, let us recall the Ten Plagues against Egypt:

The red shotglass that says "blood,"	דָם
the small plastic frog,	צְפַרְדֵעַ
the plastic praying mantis,	כִּנִּים
I coulda sworn there was a lion in here— is that Beasts?	עָרוֹב
the slide-the-squares puzzle of a verklempt cow,	דֶּבֶר
the sticky gummyhand with white spots,	שְׁחִין
the red and white bouncyball,	בָּרָד
is this a Lice or a Locust?	אַרְבֶּה
I couldn't find Darkness, which figures,	חוֹשֶׁךְ
and I lost the First Born, too, but then again	מַכַּת בְּכוֹרוֹת

    so did the Egyptians.

THE FOUR SONS AND ONE GOD-FORBID
FUTURE DAUGHTER-IN-LAW

What says the wise son? He asks: "What are these testimonies, statues, and judgments which the Eternal, our God hath commanded you?" Then thou shalt instruct him in the laws of the Passover, that a good Seder runs max 30 minutes and that, when it is his turn to be Sedermister, if Uncle Harold should run off with a shiksa half his age like his father before him, he shalt never deviate from the highlighted parts.

What says the simple son? He asks: "What is this?" Then thou shalt tell him: "What do you mean, *what is this*? It's Passover. Don't be a putz."

What says the wicked son? He asks: "What mean you by taking away my cell phone when dad can keep his?" Then thou shalt tell him: "dad is a goy, so he can play Angry Birds during Seder."

For he who hath no capacity to inquire thou must begin the narration as it is said: "go in the other room and watch the Cavs."

And what says the wise son's shiksa girlfriend? She asks: "What mean you by this service?" By the word "you," it is clear that she doth not include herself because she's a Lutheran and is taking the wise son to Easter this Sunday, and therefore was never one of us to begin with. It is therefore proper to retort upon her by saying, "It's a long story."

WE BEGIN TO ANSWER, OR MAYBE NOT

We cousins are four men—
wise, wicked, simple,
and cannot ask a question.
There is one woman—

Allison: we cousins are five.
But the Haggadah speaks
only of sons. One cousin son
now has twin baby boys—

are they sons 5 and 6?
Wise, simple, wicked,
cannot answer a question,
and two more who cannot do

much but kvetch?
    [they'll fit right in]
Or are they sons one
and two, a new generation

of Afikomen scavengers?
Where did Harold hide
the Afiko-women?
My brother and I are

Caines, not able to call
ourselves Wassermen
like everyone else.
Nobody calls himself

or herself a Wasserwoman.
As it is written on tombstones
and Bar Mitzvah kipahs
and receipts taped to deli trays:

We are Wassermen. Some of us
are also Caines. In the Book
Cain is the wicked one, so
that answers that question.

Wise is the one who made
Jewish twin babies. Wicked
are the ones who bring
goyim ladies to Seder.
Wicked are the ones who heartbreak
mothers by leaving Cleveland.

SEPARATE SEDERS:
THE EXODUS OF GRANDPA

He had a boat and a condo

He had a Lexus

He had a divorce.

Grandma had a stroke.

We tried to have a Seder

He wouldn't talk to her

"tell your mother to pass the pickles."

One year Grandpa didn't show up.

Grandpa tried to come into the family room

Rabbi Matt took him by the elbow,

and then he didn't.

and then he had a Chrysler.

The younger cousins still don't know why.

The younger cousins can guess why.

with both of them anyway.

except to look at Uncle Harold and say

We tried separate Seders.

One year much later Grandma died.

at the funeral home.

led him away.

SHULCHAN ORECH

[we eat the festive meal]

THE LANGUAGE WE GRIEVE IN IS TRAYS

What do you mean I don't like lox of course I like lox. Creamed herring maybe not, but lox, yes. A cookie tray? You shouldn't have. Here, put this in the garage with the other ones. Did Grandma like creamed herring? Mom preferred gefilete fish. Did you know gefilte fish is made of Asian Carp? It can't be. I heard on NPR you can't eat Asian Carp. A cookie tray? You shouldn't have. Here put this in the garage with the other ones. Kevin—the Catholic one!—looked up why we sit on short chairs. It's to sit closer to the deceased but I think that's gross. Yeah plus mom's up in heaven anyway. Jack's does a good dairy tray, you know? For $300 they better. $300? Mom isn't making this cheap. Are you sure you don't want to take cookies back to Kansas? A cookie tray? You shouldn't have. Here put this in the garage with the other ones. Too bad these cookies aren't kosher for Passover. Maybe Danny will take some back to Kansas. Are you writing down who brought what? Aunt Lynn's friend Rickie sent a tray. Uncle Mike's poker friends sent a tray. Alan's work friend George sent a tray. Grandma's boyfriend's daughter sent a tray. Aunt Lynn's Sunday school teacher colleagues sent a tray. Judy's officemates sent a tray. They're from a small bakery in Hudson. I like to support small business, especially ones owned by women. These Giant Eagle sugar cookies are killer. Are you sure you don't want to take some back to Kansas?

CREED

We are the Bagelox Jews.

We believe in the food from the countries
where they tried to kill our grandparents

and we will fight
      with our wallets
            to save the places
                  that serve it.

May H&H Bagels Rest in Peace.
May Essa Bagel soldier on.

We can name the top three Bagels
the top three bowls of Matzoh Ball Soup
and the top three Corned Beef Sandwiches
in Cleveland, New York, Chicago, and LA.

In Cleveland: Corky's for soup
Slyman's for Corned Beef,
Bialys for bagels and Jack's
for Shiva trays.

We believe our aunt's soup
is better than your aunt's soup.

We are not sure what we believe
about Israel—we watched Zionist
VHS in Sunday School but we read
about colonialism and genocide
at tiny colleges in the Midwest.

There are no Netanyahu sermons
in our halls, but there may be

a laminated poster of the Dome of the Rock
in our second-favorite Falafel shop
on the Upper West Side.

We are not sure what we believe
about God, but we're not atheists—

we are no unbelievers.

We believe in the exodus
God fed the Jews.

We believe in the diaspora
God feeds the Jews.

PUTTING THE "BAR" IN "BAR MITZVAH:" THE BAGELOX BOY BECOMES A MAN

Only after your cousin Jeff has taken you
to your first bar—

a tin-ceiling narrow brick Brooklyn place
called Pencil Factory,
across from an old
Pencil Factory—

only after the bartender has called you forward
[Aliyah]

to recite the words Jeff taught you to say
[Parshah] *Jameson and Ginger*

only after   [haftarah] *beer please*
[haftarah] *beer please*
[haftarah] *white Russian please*

only after you go to the apartment
behind the store where Jeff's stylish
friends sell sarongs and incense
[Oneg]

only after you have puffed and passed
[borei prei hagafen]

only after you have passed out in the cab
to the dispatcher's static litany
        [Kaddish]

only after you have woken up on Jeff's
expensive midcentury couch with flames
in your forehead
        [Ad'Vil]

can you go to Second Avenue Deli and order
        [Aliyah]
Matzoh Ball Soup

only after you've slurped the soup
        [maggid]
can you rest your head on the cool table

trying not to spit up when the waiter
brings the Corned Beef on Rye
        [hamotzi]

only after you've coughed down half
the sandwich can you wrap it in a napkin

and only after you've winced into the sun
can you descend to the sweaty L train

can you become ravenous finally
can you eat that half sandwich in two

bites and become a [Wasser]man
[bar mitzvah]

BARECH

[we say the blessing after the meal]
[third glass of wine]
[welcome Elijah the prophet]

WE RAISE THE THIRD GLASS AND SAY

This cup is for Eliyahu Hanavi, Elijah the Prophet. We open our front door to greet our honored guest and invite him to join our seder. We pray that he will return to us bringing a time of peace and freedom.

This cup is for cousin Jeff, who moved to NYC to become an architect and marry a pretty Jewish girl from Hudson and buy a cute purebred and a weekend house upstate. We open our front door to greet him and invite him to join our Seder. We pray that he will return to us, even though he probably won't.

And *this* cup is for Danny, who married a gentile and moved to Kansas to write poems about us even though he won't let us read them. Even though you can't get a health-insurance pension-plan job with an MFA. We open our front door to greet him and invite him to join our Seder. We pray that he will return to us, even though he probably won't.

And *this* cup is for Grandma, who died months before becoming a great Grandma. We open our front door to greet her and invite her to join our Seder. We pray that she will return to us, even though she probably won't. If she does, we pray that she remembers her meshuggah hearing aids.

And *this* cup is for Cousin Alan, and his twins at their first Seder. We open our front door to greet our honored guests, to welcome the ones who showed up. Let us call Uncle Harold Grandfather Harold for the first time. Let us thank God for the most precious of all his gifts: Jewish grandchildren. New Wassermen. Let us add more, subtract less. May the other cousins take a ferkakta hint.

UNCLE HAROLD'S חַיּ:
THE SEDERMEISTER'S STEPS
TO SELLING YOUR HOUSE

1. Convert the Methodist you marry,
    Raise your son in the tribe

2. When your parents divorce,
    it is your turn to be Sedermeister

3. Create the Passover Powerpoint

4. Smile while your son marries a Catholic

5. Smile at your sister's surprise baptism

6. Smile as your daughter-in-law converts

7. Sit Shiva for your wife

8. A Jack's dairy tray for the mourners

9. Keep the house on the market for

10. Months and months with no leads

11. Ask your newly Catholic sister which Saint sells houses

12. Bury The St. Joseph Home Seller Kit®
    head toward the house

13. Accept the bid

14. Move your mom into a home and another kind of home

15. Is it relief you feel when she dies,
    that it was pretty quick?

16. A Jack's dairy tray for the mourners

17. *Keep St. Joseph in a place of honor in your new home*

18. Next to the Menorah

THE FIFTH QUESTION

*"Do you have a fifth question about the Seder that
you would like to ask?"*

Why doesn't cousin Alan like Uncle Harold's
new girlfriend? Why did all our sons move away
but our daughter stayed? Who ate all the pickles
already? Does Alan still keep Playboys under his bed?
Is Maror the apple stuff or the horseradish? When
does one of the cousins host the Seder? When can
you come home and meet the twins? When is Jeff
gonna have kids? Matt, are you seeing anyone?
Allison, are you seeing anyone? Danny, when are
you gonna have kids? Are your kids gonna be Jewish?
Well, will you at least circumcise any boys?
Isn't killing the first born a bit harsh? Why does
the New York cousin like the Cavs and the Columbus
cousin like the Yankees? What's the score of the Cavs game?
What does it look like when a mountain skips like a ram?
Why are all the cousins together only at funerals?
Why does a coffee corporation sponsor Passover?
Why hasn't Danny shown us his poems?

HALLEL

[we sing songs of praise]
[fourth glass of wine]

WE RAISE THE FOURTH GLASS AND SAY

all other nights we drink as many
glasses of wine as we wish;
tonight it is a commandment unto us
to drink four—

and Aunt Lynn maybe two as her
digestion is bad enough to begin with—

and mom none, as the fruit of the vine
giveth her the migraine.

On this night thou shalt give
Cousin Matt the stink eye
as he pours forth too much
into his third glass.

On this night I suppose you can
give her some fruit of the vine
since she's the shiksa
wife now.

And on this night thou shalt, all of you
after dessert lose interest in the Seder
and rise to wash the dishes—
to see if the Cavs are winning—
to play fetch with Mitzvah—

and thus shalt thou leave
Uncle Harold to pray
and drink the fourth glass
alone.

THE WICKED SON PREPARES
TO FIND THE AFIKOMEN

Shake the Halleluyah Tambourine® and bust
out the Matzah Crumb Sweeper® because
it's Afikoman time, schmucks.

If someone else cashes in on Uncle Harold's
cold hard shekels, I will slap them with mom's Matzah
Pattern Printed Oven Mitt®. Don't think I'm kidding—

I'm packing a Star of David Swiss Army Knife® and I
am NOT afraid to use it. With last year's Afikoman
I bought a book called *But He Was Good To His Mother:*

The Lives and Crimes of Jewish Gangsters, and I've learned
a *lot.* The last thing I see before I go to bed
is my IDF Kfir C7 Fighter Jet Die Cast Model.

Call me the wicked son but since I've been able to walk
I've been 8 for 8 on the Pesach payday, even if it meant
some cousins got a Matzah Pattern Kipah® stuffed

down their ferkakta throats. I'm unstoppable like
the Waterskiing Rabbis framed on Uncle Harold's
bathroom wall. I'm plucky and determined

like Moses or Aaron or Judah Maccabe. Let me answer

your four questions right here, right now: our ancestors
schlepped outta Egypt before they could bake bread,

so now we get paid at the end of every Seder, but only
if we're fast and only if we're ruthless, No, *mom*, I will not
stop plotzing. Seder's over, festive meal is done,
it's time to part the Red Sea, it's time to run.

DAYENU
[it would have been enough for us]

If He had executed judgment upon their gods, and had not slain their first-born

Dayenu

If He had slain their first-born, and had not bestowed their wealth on us

Dayenu

If He had given us their wealth, and had not divided the sea for us

Dayenu

If He had divided the sea for us, and had not ensured the turkey didn't dry out

Dayenu

If He had kept the turkey moist, and had not brought together, like, three of the cousins this year

Dayenu

If He had brought Allison Matt and Alan, and had not converted Alan's wife

Dayenu

If He had made Alan's wife one of us and not borne her twins

Dayenu

If He had given us the twins, and had not given us the Passover Powerpoint

Dayenu

If he had given us the Passover Powerpoint and not the Rite Lite® Ten Plagues Kit

Dayenu

If he had bestowed the fun plagues upon us and had not
wrapped things up in time for the third quarter

Dayenu

For all these—alone and together—we say

Dayenu

Amen

KADDISH

*for Joyce Feinberg, Richard Gottfried, Rose
Mallinger, Jerry Rabinowitz, Cecil Rosenthal,
David Rosenthal, Bernice Simon, Sylvan Simon,
Daniel Stein, Melvin Wax, and Irving Younger who
were killed at Pittsburgh's Tree of Life Synagogue,
October 26 2018.*

*In every generation, they rise up against us
to destroy us. They* try to cut down
the Tree of Life with dogwhistles
(mouths they have, but speak not) or AR-15s.
They think the answer is armed guards.
They don't know history or *they* ignore it
(eyes they have, but see not). The Haggadah
says nothing of thoughts and prayers. It says
*In every generation each individual is bound
to regard himself as if he had gone personally
forth from Egypt.* The Haggadah asks,
in what ways are we presently slaves? I can't
imagine bondage *(praised be He).* Still,
on a day like today I watch CNN
and think *let my people go*
to synagogue without being shot.
Let my people go online without
being harassed. *Let my people* raise
a joyous middle finger every time

they try to destroy us. Though *they*
don't want to hear it *(ears they have,*
but hear not) here we are: *once we were*
slaves in Egypt and now we recline
in folding chairs around tables
loaded with food in *thy city*
Pittsburgh, *in thy city* Cleveland.
How has the story of the Exodus
inspired other revolutions? From slavery
to freedom, from sorrow to joy. Open the door,
and let thy fierce laughter *overtake them.*

Notes

"Chrissy, John, Kanye, and Kim go to Waffle House"
This poem is based on an instagram photo of Kanye West, Kim Kardashian, Chrissy Teigen, and John Legend at Waffle House.

"If the Cavs Win the NBA Title"
This poem was written before the Cavs won the NBA title.

"Song of my Suburb"
This poem owes a debt to the work of photographer Brian Ulrich.

"One Star Tripadvisor Reviews of the Memphis Bass Pro"
All of these sentences are taken from online reviews. Some are edited for clarity.

"Uncle Harold's Maxwell House Haggadah"
Most italicized text is taken from the 1986 edition of the *Maxwell House Haggadah.* Other quotes are from *A Family Haggadah II* (1997).

"Creed"
This poem owes a small debt to the song "Finger Back" by Vampire Weekend.

Acknowledgements

Some of these poems appeared in the following places, at times in alternate forms. I thank these journals:

Atticus Review ("Jaycie")

Café Review ("I Love You Detroit,")

DIAGRAM ("Gun Math")

Hobart ("Chrissy, John, Kanye, and Kim go to Waffle House," "Continental Breakfast," "The New American Dream," "Churches Replacing Stores at Euclid Square Mall (With Slideshow)," "In the Bathroom of the Renaissance Downtown," "Song of my Suburb")

The Legendary ("The Best Little Pasta Place in Florence")

Mid-American Review ("The Four Sons and the One God-Forbid Future Daughter-in-Law")

Midwestern Gothic: ("The Middle West")

Minnesota Review ("Bono Rings My Doorbell")

More than Sports Talk: ("If the Cavs Win the NBA Title" and "English 102 in Big 12 Country")

New Ohio Review: ("The Ideal Budweiser Customer Watches A Budweiser Commercial")

Rip Rap Journal ("Dinner at Applebee's With Edward Said")

TL;DR ("#UPFORWHATEVER," "Ben & Jerry's Free Cone Day," "Four Friars, Each Alike in Dignity, In Fair Washington DC")

Additionally, *Uncle Harold's Maxwell House Haggadah* was published in an altered form as a chapbook of the same name by Etchings Press.

Thanks, first, to my teachers and mentors: Phil Metres, Megan Kaminski, Dan Bourne, Karl Woelz, George Bilgere, Jennifer L. Knox, Alissa Nutting and Erika Meitner. Thanks to my poetry partners in crime: Paige Webb, Lesley Wheeler, Alyse Bensel, Dee MacElhattan, Mercedes Lucero, and Brenna Dimmig. Thanks to all the editors who advocated and supported this work, especially Aaron Burch, Paul Asta, J. Allyn Rosser, Kevin McKelvey, and Joe Lucido. Thanks also to Ian and Michael at Mason Jar Press for making this book look so good and making the first-book process painless and fun. Thank you to my family, of course for the support, but also for being such good sports.

Thank you, finally, and most of all, to Kara and Jack.

About the Author

Danny Caine is the author of the books *Continental Breakfast* (Mason Jar Press, 2019) and *El Dorado Freddy's* (collaboration with Tara Wray, Belt Publishing 2020), and the chapbook *Uncle Harold's Maxwell House Haggadah* (Etchings Press, 2017). His poetry has appeared in *Hobart, Barrelhouse, DIAGRAM, New Ohio Review*, and other places. His book reviews have appeared in *Rain Taxi* and *Los Angeles Review*. He has an MFA in poetry from the University of Kansas and an MA in English from John Carroll University. He hails from Cleveland and lives in Lawrence, Kansas where he owns the Raven Book Store.

More at dannycaine.com.

More books from Mason Jar Press

How to Sit
memoir/fiction by Tyrese Coleman

Broken Metropolis
fiction anthology edited by Dave Ring

I Am Not Famous Anymore
poetry by Erin Dorney

The Bong-Ripping Brides of Count Drogado
fiction by Dave K

Not Without Our Laughter
poetry by Black Ladies Brunch Collective

Notes From My Phone
memoir by Michelle Junot

Nihilist Kitsch
poetry by Matthew Falk

Learn more at masonjarpress.xyz.